evolution psalms

Saint Julian Press

Poetry

Praise for evolution psalms

Unsparingly personal and objectively incisive, Tayve Neese's poems reverberate with the disintegration, on the one hand, of a marriage, on the other, of our planet as, indifferent to our bequest, to all that is sacred, we stagger toward extinction. The poet's registers echo those of "The Tui of New Zealand," which "has two voice boxes / making two / distinct songs: // one blossoms / sorrow, / one reeks / of joy," ("I Know This Polarity"), embracing everything in between. On her path to reconciliation and redemption, she sings the natural and the supernatural—enigmatic, palliative, maternal— as the pungent, sinuous lyrics of *Evolution Psalms* affirm our provenance in the primeval.

~ Bhisham Bherwani
The Second Night of the Spirt
and *The Circling Canopy*

Tayve Neese's *Evolution Psalms* are, indeed, poetic praises to nature's evolving creatures in all their glory. However, this collection could also be named "The Psalmist's Evolution." Instead of crying out to the silence of King David's patriarchal God that has deserted him in the Old Testament, these psalms find a holy presence in the "gaseous beckon" of a "vibrating star" that "gives some direction," in a "baby whale thinking [a] yacht its mother," and in a "sea snail egg [that] "grew and hatched inside a boy's knee." These organic connections between all things stand in contrast to the false assumption that the sacred and the profane were ever separate. Psalmist Neese asserts, "it is my body in which you make your home." These poems reach down into our collective unconscious. Reading them will manifest their truth in our bodies.

~ Terry Lucas
Dharma Rain

Tayve Neese's laconic, dynamic, rhythmically impeccable poems evolve with the determination of banyan tree roots, bound only by the mesmerizing pulse of metamorphosis – skeletal, igneous, stellar, emotional. Their tapestry is filled with scale-defying wonders – a horseshoe crab, a feather, or a molecule of salt – relying on each other for space to coil around, to fork through, to nest in; representing love itself in its incessant earthly movement. *Evolution Psalms* is an unforgettable book capable of refocusing and refreshing the reader's vision.

~ Irina Mashinski – Co-Editor
The Penguin Book of Russian Poetry

evolution psalms

Poems

by

Tayve Neese

SAINT JULIAN PRESS
HOUSTON

Published by
SAINT JULIAN PRESS, Inc.
2053 Cortlandt, Suite 200
Houston, Texas 77008

www.saintjulianpress.com

ISBN-13: 978-1-955194-01-3
Library of Congress Control Number: 2021952058

Cover Art: Frontexto: "Los días oscuros" 380
By Octavio Quintanilla

❖

FOR SAGE & BELLA

CONTENTS

"No poetic phantasy
but a biological reality,

a fact: I am an entity
like a bird, insect, plant

or a sea-plant cell;
I live; I am alive;

take care, do not know me,
deny me, do not recognize me,

shun me; for this reality
is infectious—ecstasy."

— H.D. *from part IX, "The Flowering of the Rod"*

evolution psalms

IN SPRING, MY DENIAL STILL
WILL NOT THAW

I walk up the mountain,
come upon skull
and ribs of a mule deer.

A purple larkspur
sprouts from its left hoof.

A thorny weed
grows from its right eye.

Foliage touches its bones
in blessing
and I wonder how it died.

I walk down the mountain,
tell myself,
I am not the bullet.
I am not the edge
of a knife.

I CAN FEEL THE WORLD ABOUT TO FALL

off the edge of a precipice.

The hermit crab makes
its home in a plastic

doll's head. The swan
          has gathered grocery
sacks as nest
          to lay her empty eggs.

An orca carried her

dead calf above
the waterline for seventeen days

because her grief
is deeper than the Pacific.

          I know you don't want

this poem void of dancing
bears and circuses.

          You want cotton candy,
train rides around

the zoological park. You want
          elephant rides, carnival tunes, dogs who

never bite or bark.

HE SAYS, IT'S SO SHALLOW

living in the subtropics
with all those screaming

flowers,

to which I say—
maybe,

but all those stories
from feathered throats,

all those marsupials
hidden in foliage

near sulfur water,

murex shells teaching
wisdom of spirals,

red-yellow-black
snake singing,

shed, shed,

that's deep —
think philosophy

of banyan roots'

spread.

I'M IN NEED OF ONE GOOD EYE OR A TELESCOPE

because a star
vibrates—gaseous beckon

pulses through October to give
some direction.

Rings of Saturn, auspicious,
mean union or noose.

Moons of Jupiter, aligned,
mean evolution,

that I should become a forest
to house songs of a bower bird,

& let my roots reach through clay,
past aquifers of this earth.

I BELIEVE IN CHAKRAS

spinning over hearts,
genitals,

I believe bee dances
make them diminutive

cartographers,

our dead appear as scent
to attend their funerals,

tankas and sonnets
are a species of orchids,

trauma lodged in DNA
will become an echo,

mercy is a snake's skin
left for us to borrow.

HARVEST

Bled for our tests on coagulation,
living horseshoe crabs are kept by the thousands
in warehouses to gather their ice blue gels.

We pluck them from shallow ocean waters,
we pluck them from the February shore.
Their desire to mate an unshakable spell

to leave strands of salty eggs— their demise.
Hung over glass bottles, tubed, pierced, tied,
drained, the primordial keep us alive.

SEA STARS MYSTERIOUSLY DISAPPEARING ALONG THE PACIFIC COAST

Orange County Register, May 2nd 2014

Sub-tidal zones, warming, turn dark
as echinoderm arms dissolve.

Limbs losing rigidity

is no magic-trick,
no fault of ocean's rough ebb,

salt. It is massive die-off.

Aquatic stars, their rock-clinging
constellations vanish as comet tail spark.

BABY WHALE SEEMS TO THINK YACHT IS ITS MOTHER

AP Press, August 19th 2008

I also replace her with stern, bow,
for the primal lull of her rhythmic

rocking. Lost, I've spent a lifetime swimming
rip-tides in the wrong direction,

floating in the soft chasm of a lover's neck
listening for a heartbeat promising nourishment.

My whole life a compass searching for her
scent meant to bring me back to her arms, breast.

Under green eyes of strangers, I wait for the familiar
sea-glint of approval over my ironed dress,

follow the closest floating object to avoid undertow
and drift.

SONG OF THE LIONESS

for the stolen brides, from AP press 2005

Three circled the pulp of her face,
paws leaving a braided path in the Ethiopian
grass as amber as their bristle.

They kept her from
more fingers, rotten breath.
It was the deep movement
in the girl's throat,
the swallowing of weeping,
not the blood between her legs,
that sent pink tongues,
open jaws into unison calling

and the men who had tried
to beat the girl into marriage
ran for dried sticks, hid behind trees
until the feline voices of knives
pushed them from the girl
as lovely as a gazelle.

Turning like suns
the cats warmed her bruises,
sat near her broken
arms, her crooked ribs
until her mother came,
recognizable by scent
just as much by the sound
of tears *tap-tapping*
onto what was withered
below her searching feet.

Dressed in white,
she watched them
before they left—
the three breathing

over her child,
the exchange of air
in and out
of warm wide lungs.

I KNOW THIS POLARITY

The Tui of New Zealand
has two voice boxes
making two
distinct songs:

one blossoms
sorrow,
one reeks
of joy.

Under beak,
her white tuft feather
is as abrupt as earth
from sky.

From the branches
of Kōwhai,
two selves
she hides.

RADIOACTIVE BOARS ARE ROAMING AROUND GERMANY

Smithsonian Magazine, Sept 2, 2014

Plowing field with snout, they sniff out truffle,
root, leave poisonous dark bristles

on twigs. Tusks, over generations,
shorten for lack of need.

No arrows threaten ribs, no scent
of hunters chasing sows to bleed

them from their throats.
Litters are born, each small fetus

misshapen before birth,
ill formed bones, or lacking hoof.

Our disaster—their savior from blade,
our uranium—allowing sounder's growth.

EVOLUTION PSALMS

Praise the slow crack of bone
    sprouting feathers, marrow
    lightening in preparation for sky.

Praise the fish's desire to slip
    from salt water to sand,
    the invertebrate's flexion, spine.

⁂

When finned things grew foot,
when gill gave to lung—

they'd had enough of brine,
wanted only ground, dirt.

When foot begot feather, and feather begot fur,

and when those covered in fur grew
fingers, opposable thumbs,

they saw their reflections in lakes, ponds.

Below swam the scaled and tailed,
who they lifted, let swirl against palms—

silver mouths caressing their fingers,
hands remembering original mothers.

⁂

Let the righteous rejoice in the hand, once aquatic fin
   which, like a bud blossomed
   by cell's heat, mutation.

⁜

Wind chiseled
the face of homo erectus.

The frontal brow receded
from its caress.

Cerebellum thickened,
expanded, thought ignites.

Synapses unstoppable
flame, holy light.

⁜

Teeth have forgotten foliage,
devour inland hooved flesh,

They are weary of crustaceans.
Their equilibriums shun

the ocean's hymn and ebb.
Skies, not seas, keep their departed,
now gods must have talons or two legs.

⁜

Lo, the neck of the animal
  grew speckled, reaching
for the highest leaf.
  Hunger contorted muscle,
desire for chlorophyll's sweet
  elongating bone, nerve sheath.

           ⚛

Gracious is the dome shell
  over soft limbs of silent reptiles
  with no need for song.

Grief and darkness delivered outward bone
  as swaddle and refuge
  from enemies' incisors, wrongs.

           ⚛

Let light illumine the atavism,
  the whale's genetic code for growing legs,
  the foul's one missing protein
  for erupting teeth.
Let light illumine the human tail
  upon embryo swirling at seven weeks.

           ⚛

Praise the mammal with wings, the reptile
  that gives live birth to her young.
Praise the puzzle of fossil, shift of bone,
  mandible stretch and recession,

three toes turned hooves,
  our single-cell origin
  before oxygen's collision.
Trust in the flesh's alteration, life-force's urn,
  our salvation.

INSIDE BOY'S KNEE, SEA SNAIL EGG GREW AND HATCHED

Huffington Post, August 16th 2013

in a womb of blood and pus
its muscular foot gentle against patella's

bend. Such moisture, warmth, slowed
its mucous gland. Children, be certain–

moths erupt from the center
of hands, hummingbirds nest

under the safety of your fourth rib.
The golden coqui of your dream

still swirls in cerebellum' egg.

TO THE GODS OF EVOLVING THINGS

from a line after Matt Mauch

When the fin had no choice
        but to turn into finger,
                the skull nub into antler,

what faith have you left us with
                        when alteration forward
        is as solid as copper?

Perhaps, the unused ranges
        of our voice-box
                will give way to only one

        monotonous note,
because in this lifetime
        we have all stopped singing.

Since we forget to hear the talking
        of trees, one to the other,
        trunks swirling in aria,

                roots' muffled stretch through soil,
        will you unravel the nautilus
of our inner ear?

The body we are now
will not be our body
                in the future.

What need have we of tongues
              unless we relearn how to speak
to one another.

What need of teats,
unless we remember
the sacredness of the mother.

MOTHER CHANT

Birth mother flint
mother old mother water mother poor mother woven
mother Mary mother sick mother step
mother Lilith mother stick mother stone mother neon
mother Jewish mother empty mother MILF mother Danu
mother your mother my mother bourbon mother Durga
mother fat mother first mother Kali mother shamed
mother bud mother gene mother rib mother spider
mother Queen mother teen mother native mother
feathered mother iron mother covered mother naked
mother broken mother earth mother barren mother sly
mother spiral mother green mother sow mother chosen
mother Sappho mother grandmother dirty mother left
mother sacred mother rust mother milk mother buried
mother skin mother moon mother dry mother thorn
mother blind mother rune mother fertile mother Lucy
mother swamp mother you mother I mother death
mother arrow mother

ABBEY IN HARVARD, MASSACHUSETTS

Where you have built your temple and bell,
larkspur grows between stones.

Your hill slides into valley, rounded
and rolling like a birthing woman.

The green bulge of land resembles a full
breast, the long plateau, a thigh,

more evocative than the statue
of Mary in your garden,

her palms turned up
give heat of skin to only sky,

her fertile hips
and abdomen, you hide.

ARACHNE

You boasted of your hand at spindle—

now you spin all hours and seasons,
travel on eight elegant legs.

Do calves remember grit of the Aegean,
thistle praising two ankle joints?

Do you remember Phthonus's arms artfully
slipping around your maiden's waist.

No one out of jealousy turned him into serpent,
and no one remembers your amber hair—

how on hot days it tightened into locks
resembling lamb's wool.

ATHENA'S OWL

Athena's admirer tried not to despise
its gray feathers reluctant for flight.

He imagined its black eyes
a cool well on the hottest nights

of his desire, the water where he drowned.
He tried not to hate the silent raptor,

thought it easy for him to devour,
it having no incisors, knife,

only talons, spotted wings making home
on his beloved's olive shoulder.

BOW-MAKER

Because she was so beautiful,
he made the goddess of war

quivers from trunks of olive trees,
so that in her reluctance to send points

into flesh of her enemies,
once loved, she could imagine

the fashioned arrows as peace-offerings

lodged into quick beating ventricles,
hamstrings, caps of knees.

Once felled, they slept on the ground,
larkspur creeping toward their clavicles,

and the bow-maker thought *how lovely*

to be surrounded by such flowers
caressed by her aim and fingers,
to be taken by branches that sprout black fruits

whose twigs are carried in the mouths of doves.

BARBARO, GONE DOWN

Colt kissed by Mercury on each hoof, it was Achilles
who felt your plight, knew the shame of tumble.

Once, your femurs were willows. Once, your ligaments
brought flight to flank and mane.

How quickly flesh swivels, unravels like skein.
Unable to withstand saddle, leather of bridle,

there is no more quiver of your soft ear, debtors'
cheer igniting gallop, rhythm of holy muscle.

But the ground knows where you first broke cantor.
Though pasture is long fallow, grass and seeds still
tremble.

NO TIGER'S CORPSE

Because fear is striped feline,
her rumble, rhythm of lung
how you've measured your days,

forget the elegant arrow aimed
at her fourth rib,
seek absence of bloodshed,

wound, wait for snap of twig
as golden irises broaden
from pinpoints in your direction.

A bristled pelt over your shoulder
has too much heft, weight.
Conquer her with outstretched hand,

offer her your violet jugular,
welcome her embrace.

WHY, EGO, WHAT BIG TEETH YOU HAVE

Your incisors glint, reflect
the moon and my own heart-shaped face.

You lead me down dead-end brick
alleyways whispering of the sea.

I turn child enticed by rainbow
of your hard candies, your promised sweet,

though my tongue never tastes.

You talk of poppies in the deep
of winter, praise the loveliness

of my moth-bitten woolen cape.

I HAVE GLANCED THE UNDERBELLY

of the night   where the softest
truth hides at teat,

bulbous eyes shut, hairless pink
body a single tremor.

Let it fatten in its own
time, grow incisors

and yellow claws
that clamor *up*

down up– music
in the drywall.

KARMA IS A BLADED

boomerang

sniffing you out

over decades.

Let its sting

be your

awakening.

Let it clip

the heads

of poppies

for your

chipped

glass

vase.

STAMPEDE

What thought requires exile?

Glint of his violet hair.

Honeysuckle fingers.

Decade's grief turns fodder

under trample of hooves

flanks of willing cattle—

memory pounded to powder

over cerebellum's gravel.

THREE THOUGHTS ON
DIFFRACTION

Think of light as marbles rolling in all directions.
Think of marbles stuck in perpetual motion
unable to pass through grate, or without force, change
trajectory.

Think of light as light. How it gives, twists,
bends— refracts from a central point with no hesitation.
Its spreading outward from source— its salvation.

Think of light as bodies, think of bodies
as light able to depart from one another with ease—
(illuminated. golden.) attracting bulbous eyes of new honey
bees.

MITOSIS

did you hear about the rusted lovers
when reaching for one another

their fingers collapsed into dust of iron ore
their divorce caused a tsunami, ripped

sea-oats from the west facing shore
no, wait— you say there was just a ripple

their splitting far from nuclear
their parting nothing like the Red Sea

but slow, as one cell dividing

smooth, painlessly

MY GIRLS, NOW ELECTRONS,

spin between our homes.
They keep our bond covalent,
keep our centers, pulsing
with resentment and dust,

neutral. They are the slight
connection I will never sever.
Their return, needed electric charge.
Their leaving, nucleus ill to adjust.

1998

My house built near the grove never filled with fruit,
smelled of smoke, but light through dusted windows
made bright squares across your torso,
                your fingers, expectant.

Linoleum peeled at floor's corners,
rust took door handles, hinge,
   but your hands, mine, enmeshed.

We cannot go back to nights coved with tin
roof, our midnight rooster's untimely call under the moon,
                our perfection of touching—
                        trembling, trembling— new.

BACK TO THE COLONNADE

We married here, danced
on marble swirls resembling koi,

ate guava cheesecake the color
of our stucco house, Everglades

heart-of-pine floor, fireplace
that held only nesting sparrows.

Their small echoes reverbed
off the red brick, gathered downy feathers

where there never was ember.
Winters were signaled

by miniature colored bulbs
woven through palm fronds.

All marriages should begin
in tropical places filled with orchids,

sweet plantains, where men
and women love

like hurricanes.

WE WERE BEACHCOMBERS

nautilus lovers, hands sifting
grains for sharks' teeth.

Tides left us beach-glass, jelly-fish,
jagged limbs of coral reef.

Once, we both trusted ocean's
foam, sand bar's relief

after hours of treading water
in the deepest part of the sea.

BAPTISM AT TABACON

Thermal waters over igneous
stone,
we submerge ourselves
up to shoulders,

honeymooners leaving behind
uni-lives.
Our eyes level with bromeliads,
one another.

Unknown flora fills jungle.
Unfathomable depth
of magma—
heat from volcano.

WIFE

Carcass of horseshoe crab,
legs collapsed from ancient weight
of carrying her burden of primordial shell

over her soft body. To throw off her armor,
what would take: a many-legged kindred
prizing her pearled eggs, or a return

to the beginning, before evolution
of carapace, pincers, before she grew barbed
tail for necessary protection?

ANOTHER ME

is still in Coral Gables
living in the stucco house

with its arched door,
and it is only the green flocks

of parrots who are screaming.

You are a placid ocean.
You are painting a room yellow.

We are waiting for our child
to be born, our daughter

turning circles inside of me.

She is a golden fish. Her sister wears a pink dress,
twirls to the east and on the Chicago

brick, she teaches the soon-born
how to spin, and through my flesh

they are swirling together.

The parrots settle in bamboo,
and every living thing waits

for our world to begin
as you color the drywall, ready a room

in which we all will live

and sit at an unfinished
pine table.

WHEN YOU LEAVE YOUR LOVER, LEAVE HIM IN A CLUSTER

of pines with nothing but needles,

and one flightless raven

making a nest of baubles

turned to rust. When you leave,

remember a backward glance

means salt, indecision.

Look west toward prairie,

lure of grassy horizon

that also resembles the sea.

AFTER YEARS OF MARRIAGE

the heart is a koi
pond lined with
decayed   scales

a startled and starving
gazelle   April's

blue egg
stopped pulsing
in a nest of poplar
twigs   twine

what do you do
with the emaciated

draw it out with biscuit
crumbs   wine
leave a salt-lick
in a fallow field   let another

plant seed   wait
for withered harvest's

yield?

SHE SNUCK AWAY FROM THE MARRIAGE

a wounded marsupial baring its needled
teeth. She feigned dormancy, but did not sleep.

The familiar alcove of his neck, no longer
her resting place, she was forced to nest

with what had been discarded—hearts
in tatters, hearts taken by atrophy, hearts

only a muscle moving blood mindlessly.

Where to find warmth, its constancy?
She turns from familiar rafters, attics,

away from former domesticity.

She follows a slow scent to her origins,
looks to those who

knew her as another creature, pre-puberty

when she was just a girl, just a girl,
the world before her all ocean, nautilus, salt.

How to mend the wound he left?
Balm of another,

and another.

Foreign fingers fumbling over her
mandible, chest. How to mend the wound?

Let it fester. Let it lead her in a southern direction
toward home, toward the sea.

It was there they marveled over a pair of barred owls
under waxen magnolia leaves.

He has forgotten all memory of it. The
swirl of koi in their hidden pond. He has forgotten

all memory of it. Golden scales, canopy of oaks,
warmth of her auburn hair—gone.

Once, their lives there were small, hinged like a bivalve,
one half to the other
holding tightly to a single muscle.

She no longer hoards the marriage like sea-glass:

something dull turned treasure,
something broken made smooth.

WHAT THE CONCH SPOKE

when she was lost
in sea dunes with only the bite of sun—

Forgive,
it echoed from its pink chamber.

Let the tide take him. The sky,
the ocean is broad,

begs for your surrender.
Ahead of you, brine, green-blue

water, a tern held up by nothing
but its own feathers.

Suspended on wind, the alchemy
of your life

to fall in love with.

I WILL REMOVE THE
KNEE-LENGTH SKIRT

leave it behind to tremble as husk,
but not as another relic

for my daughters' tender fingers.

Let me be covered by something moss colored,
archaic, live

where no automobile ever travels,
where no fiber-optic cable ever threads.

I will make a home in the green hills,
leave behind the telephone

and speak only to stones
who have lost desire to be constellations,

who shun dominion in leather-soled shoes
and neckties. I will forget

the names of the days,
articulate only seasons, the angle of light,

whittle down my language to an arrow tip
for survival.

Let everything else become hieroglyph.
Let the morning hours come and go

as I mimic a field's longing
to be filled with many roots,

become free from being shaped like a wire
hanger on which a man

will hang his drab coat.

MONOGAMY IN SPRINGTIME

the world all root, pistil
thorn—

chlorophyll's beacon, sonic—
leaves in the garden are drunk

gum-weed's yellow centers
rival the sun

legs of pollinators ache
for every gold-dusted stamen

but touch only one

A BOY I ONCE KNEW

was so auburn and speckled.
He wielded a hammer, squared

off window boxes for each pane,
painted the wood green,

planted coral impatience
and in each direction

through my glass
there were petals.

In my mind, he is still grasping
a hammer, smelling

of sweat and cedar,
laying down plank

for this wobbling dock
of my life that has carried me

over its murky currents.
I can hear his iron

hammer in rhythm
as he lays out the splintered

cypress I travel across,
and all other men's faces,

their perfect angular jaws,
their robin egg eyes,

will be measured against
the beauty of his clenched knuckles.

DOMINION

its tongue wet my neck, my thighs

but I would not lie down

hand
a giant blade
          against cheekbone
I told myself its chill was

just snow just snow

fingers pried
         from my throat
I spoke, octaves

         swallowed by purple rivers—

years tumbled
         and the same tongue

searched me out again, said
         hush, hush
         and for punishment

sent boys I loved
to war

BOMBS DO NOT FALL

as flowers—poppies
in a red shower, or like

daisies covering the rich
and poor. The soil is ready,

takes shattered limbs,
children singing at

their mothers' hems.

MINNEAPOLISBRUNSWICKBAGHDAD

one
thousand
beveled
prayers
for
one
thousand
glass-blown
children
have
passed
one
thousand
faceted
mothers'
translucent
lips

now what?

ONCE, I OWNED A TAURUS .35

slept with it under my left shoulder.
Once, its cold weight carried me
through the night hours
as my only
anchor.

I would dream of hands
at my throat, semen
burning my thigh, and awaken
to the barrel and bullets
humming their leaden
lullaby.

Did you know that midnight
still smells of jasmine
when fear takes root in the aorta,
that the sound of a single
cricket can carry you through
one night as long as October?

Listen, I've shot a .357 magnum,
a shotgun. Both left a ringing
in my right ear as Blue Label
cans fell to the clay below.
I've seen a pygmy rattler
go limp with rat shot,
its elegant body made hollow
from iron beads.

For months, from quarter moon
to quarter, the pistol remained
statuesque, trigger aching to be
pulled, its arc caressed
by my reluctant finger.

When the world was all thorns,
when the sound of drunken
men laughing made my mandible
clench, tighten, I owned a gun
and it had the voice of a Siren.

HOW TO SUTURE THE WOUNDS THAT FESTER OVER YOUR UMBILICAL AND THIRD EYE

chant ghazal-like lullabies

PICKING BLACKBERRIES WITH
MY DAUGHTER SAGE

May's bitter fruit—
don't mask it with
sugar

this is the tenor of early
pulp and early pain

take it cradle it
like a dark-eyed

newborn
until it has no choice
but sleep again

AUNT ALMA IN OCTOBER

Tuesday's recorded message—
her voice a fogged mirror
of my own mother's,

the same brass inflections,
the same staccato clearing
of her throat

upon thought's completion,
her upstate New York accent
gone as flat as stretches

of Florida's salt-marshes,
the subtle lilt of deflation
from one marriage, two,

love gone awry like poison ivy,
that when I heard Alma say:
The news said it's snowing up there,

I forgot about the ashes
between the wool and cotton
in my closet.

WHAT'S GONE MISSING IN THIS
AGE OF SATELLITES & VIRUSES

the last telephone booth
which stood empty for two decades,

housed 1980's graffiti.

Once, from this spot, while drunk,
I spoke to my lover at dusk,

watched the park's carousel
make its eternal circle.

In a storm I called my mother,
now ash, from this metal

box shaped like a coffin
for a wealthy man.

I hear there is still one phone booth
in Japan where people

talk to their dead,
but it is the living who need

to listen when I say
they took the phone booth

and the old carousel
with its painted horses,

shelters of my former life
made of music, voices.

MILKING THE COW

Weight of her hands on my hands,

the length of her body,
engulfing my child
body like a pearl

as we held the udder
together, the scent of hay,
soil and animal,

my mother's skin.

What nourishes isn't ever milk,
but rhythm—
the *pull* and *squeeze*

passed parent to daughter,

flesh teaching flesh.
This is what we turn over
during the hollow years.

NORTH TO BONAVENTURE

for Emma's Unveiling

Sulfur-sweet marshes
I cross to find
you, plot, stone.

Currents are slow,
run south. Brittle
grasses lean north,
pointing my way home
to Savannah.

Egrets
as angular as blades
rise from marsh roots
that search deep
through mud, clay

past moisture
and mollusks
to a place that is
still and dry,
impossible to fathom
in this place of tides.

I've always crossed
water on my way to you—

the Satilla, Jerico,
and Ogeechee grasses
as beige and giving
as your belly
where I rested my head
in Tybee's rope
hammocks.

Even now,
for only your echo,
I travel over
this steady rhythm
of low bridges.

SCATTER ME AT BONAVENTURE

close to the river near an oak root
in proximity to the Minkovitzes,

Friedmans—

my loved ones who sifted tides
for sand dollars, hung sugar water

for ruby-throated omens,

those whose fingers pulled aqua
colored threads turning pillows

into gardens.

Scatter me near my namesake
sleeping under a sharp triangular star

of David,

by gardenias, pink screaming
azaleas, Spanish moss above

the stone of Conrad Aiken.

Play bagpipes to remember
Annie Howard's green tartan.

Make a knot

of my ash—between two waxy
leafed magnolias—

in a Celtic Dara pattern.

WE ARE ALL CRUSOE IN THE SLANT LIGHT

of August   the pebble falls into the well

and makes no sound   the crow on the wire

loosens no feather for luck   this loneliness—

a vacuum   without dust   we take

to counting   our own fingers   exponentially

we take to reading   the same James

Dickey poem each Tuesday   a single meme —

our digital connection   with no witness

of our blue-light salvation

HYMN FOR HOW FAR ASTRAY
WE HAVE ROAMED

Farther than the stone in the farthest jetty.
Farther than the bourbon bottle

from the schizophrenic's hand.
We are scattered seeds, our angry roots

filling every inch of soil.
We live in chrome, are drunk on oil.

One small mite from a downy feather
in the microchip—we're a nation

of hazmat suits, Lysol.
We wave our wands, unravel evolution's toil.

Poof, poof. The long necks of giraffes
replaced with telephone poles,

the marsupial's pouch with expanding balloons.
We are nothing but costume   and Bakelite.

Isn't that nice? Isn't that darling?   The plastic jars
in which we save our pennies—

maracas to which we jitterbug,
and dance the Charleston.

TO THOSE OF US IN SOOTY CITIES

who wander streets of piss and chrome
rushing through alleyways
as antibodies in blood,

what glitter-dome will you look to in longing
wishing the air vodka scented with a twist
of lime.

Our pigeons are omens. Our Bichon Frises,
relics of feral lives.

Urbanites, we survive on bleach
and fish bones shaped into needles
that sew closed our eyes.

Skyscrapers are not volcanoes,
our clairvoyance gone under the rubber
of taxi wheels.

Oh, enormous city, you are no swirling galaxy,
but stuffed thick with churches and steeples.

You are a thrush-covered mouth of an infant
suckling from a Baker-acted nipple.

WITHOUT ROD OR STAFF IN THE AGE OF SATELLITES & VIRUSES

I sleep sheltered by nothing
but shadow,

drink water from a ladle
offered from no one's hand.

Along the muddy slope
of the river where no man stands,

even the wind does not touch
my uncovered shoulders.

QUARANTINE DREAM #4

I live inside the chamber
of the nautilus,

hide from wind, sun.

In the age of satellites,
and viruses,

confined to
pearlized room,

I sink, submerge,

follow Fibonacci
sequence

with my lungs.

THE PLACE OF LONGING IS BLUE

filled with a bower bird's

string, lint,

a bottlecap left

as a noise maker

akin to a cymbal—

is filled with lost downy

feathers, discarded

pieces of cobalt

bottles— shattered

treasure.

LOVE POEM IN THE AGE OF SATELLITES & VIRUSES

Oh Paloma, do you love me
the way I love this ash-heap
of a country
where neckties are scepters?

Do you love me
the way I love a nation
that buzzed with child-song
on my tongue like magic
trick although we tremble
under nuclear eyes.

And what is love, if not one
tired nurse placing an IV
in the limp arm of the beloved
we work so hard to keep
from flatlining.

Some days, your love rusts
free the anchor.
Some days, your love
is a field of poppies
on which I get stoned.

On Tuesdays, you say *goodnight*,
two syllables not spoken,
typed, and the brass-lock
on my heart, (yes, metaphysical heart), leaps
from my bone.

I AM A HALF

century, a banyan
with many wicked and merciful roots.

Lost in my own mantra
of ring-count,

parrots screech. Bats hollow a deep

hole. Still, it is my body
in which you make your home.

I smell your axe blade thick with sap.
Already, I hear you think

of kindling.

Ancient, what season have I not
seen go sour

when all I wanted was a field
trembling with violet

stamens.

ETYMOLOGY/ENTOMOLOGY

When I was a girl,
my grandfather watched me linger

   over golden insects
   tracking their diminutive

movements and stature.
Maybe you'll grow up

   to be an entomologist, he said,
   which lodged itself

   in my brain as a pearly egg,
   although with some error

in cerebellum's cipher.
Now I study words

   as ants meandering
   across my paper,

each one with its own
mandible, thorax chamber.

ADVICE TO MY YOUNGER-SELF

after Alicia Ostriker

Imagine yourself naked,
void of tweed jacket,

velvet patches
at the elbow, void of gold

wired glasses. Forget Fitzgerald,
the glory days of Paris. Anchor

yourself to a room, a table. Ask Dickinson
to make you humble. There is thunder

in your throat. Your fingers tremble
with sound, but you are just a blue-bell

making song from your small
stamen, you are a primitive

clay bowl from which another
may never drink.

Still be the bowl.
Still be the flower.

ADMIRATION OF TWO INFLECTIONS OF THE MOURNING DOVE

What need do they have of lacey
tongue:

one call says *fear*,
the other *love*.

What need of words
chiseled to stones,

chants and hymns
to sleeping gods?

Their eyes— thresholds.
Their throats give way—

just two notes,
two things to say.

(SELF) FORGIVENESS COMES AS A GREEN SNAKE

in the overgrowth
of untended vegetation

coils into scaled
circle its pupils

yellowed over what
is unpardoned

until it sheds its skin
souvenir

of dead keratin
cells   mulch

for next summer's
gardens

ACCEPTANCE

I am content in these diminutive
rooms, drink tea

from my chipped porcelain cup
as sun touches green

vines and trees.

Although I still wonder why paper
smells more like desire

than the calloused palm
of a lover, I can mark the day

I crossed the point of no turning back.
There was nothing

more than the sound of rain

on palmetto leaves,
scent of salt and sulfur.

Oh, life of my own, thank you.

You came as if rambling

through fiddle-head ferns
over mud-rich soil,

unbeckoned, surefooted.

ACKNOWLEDGEMENTS

Cordella: "A Boy I Once Knew," "Upon Stealing My Neighbor's Peaches," "Acceptance"

Diode: "Evolutions Psalms," "Radioactive Boars Are Roaming Around Germany"

Ethel: "What the conch spoke"

MiGoZine: "Without rod or staff in the age of satellites & viruses," "Quarantine #4"

Nostos: "Mitosis," "To the gods of evolving things"

Not The Time To Be Silent Anthology (An art's response anthology to the pandemic in Ireland) "What's gone missing in the age of satellites & viruses"

Open: Journal of Arts and Letters: "Milking the Cow"

Pirene's Fountain: "In spring, still my denial will not thaw," "We are all Crusoe in this slant light of August"

Silence: "I can feel the world about to fall," was longlisted for the Vice Chancellor's International Poetry Prize at the University of Canberra in Australia.

Vox Populi: "He says, *it's so shallow*," "I believe in chakras"

Many thanks to the editors who included my work: Aileen Cassinetto, Sara Lefsyk, Patty Paine, Megan Merchant, Ciaran O'Driscoll, Siobhan Potter, Michael Simms, Shane Strange, Cutter Streeby, Jeff Streeby, and Lawrence Tjernell. Thank you to Alicia Ostriker, Bhisham Bherwani, Terry Lucas, Irina Mashinski, and Matt Mauch. Much respect to the foremothers, Anne Sexton and H.D. Thank you to Ron Starbuck for giving *evolution psalms* a home with Saint Julian Press. Gratitude!

NOTES

p. 18 "To the gods of evolving things," is inspired by the poem "In addition to watching a football game none of our teams are playing in," by Matt Mauch.

p.45 "I Will Remove the Knee-length Skirt," is inspired by a compilation of Anne Sexton's poems from *The Complete Poems: Anne Sexton* (Mariner Books).

p.72 "Advice to My Younger Self," is inspired by a compilation of Alicia Ostriker's poems from *The Old Woman, the Tulip, and the Dog* (Pitt Poetry) and other poems.

ABOUT THE AUTHOR

Tayve Neese's work has appeared in journals and anthologies around the United States and abroad including *The Paris Review (online edition)*, *Comstock Review*, *Fourteen Hills*, and *diode*. Nominated for the Pushcart Prize; her work was also longlisted for the 2019 University of Canberra Vice Chancellor's International Poetry Prize in Australia. Her full-length collection of poems *Blood to Fruit* was published in 2015 and was a semi-finalist for the Able Muse Book Award. *Locust*, a full-length collection of poems, is forthcoming from Salmon Poetry. *Evolution Psalms* was a finalist for the Hudson Poetry Prize from Black Lawrence Press. Neese is Co-founder and Co-executive Editor of Trio House Press and Primary Editor of *The Banyan Review*, an international, online journal. Neese currently resides on a barrier island off the coast of Florida.

Visit her web page at www.tayveneese.com for more information.

Type Settings & Fonts:

PAPYRUS – Papyrus
PERPETUA TILTING MT
GARAMOND – Garamond

www.ingramcontent.com/pod-product-compliance
Lightning Source LLC
Chambersburg PA
CBHW030050100426
42734CB00038B/995